WOMEN SPEAK TO GOD:
The Prayers and Poems of Jewish Women

WOMEN SPEAK TO GOD:
THE PRAYERS AND POEMS OF JEWISH WOMEN

Edited by

Marcia Cohn Spiegel
and
Deborah Lipton Kremsdorf

WOMAN'S INSTITUTE FOR CONTINUING JEWISH EDUCATION
San Diego, California

Woman's Institute for Continuing Jewish Education
4079 - 54th Street, San Diego, CA 92105

Copyright © 1987 Woman's Institute for Continuing Jewish Education.

First Printing   1987
Second Printing 1989

Library of Congress Card Number: 86-51498
ISBN 0-9608054-6-X

Printed in the United States of America

Dedication

This book is dedicated to all of the women who never prayed because they felt their prayers would not be heard.

Thou must hear us, Oh God.
From of old the term "prayer" was given
To monologues of the soul.
Words ordained with rigor,
Or words that well up, rising
From the depths of the soul,
Painfully formulated,
Clumsily murmured;
Humble prayers
That must be heard, God.

Myriam Kubovy, "Monologues with God"
Translated from the French by Alicia Jurado

Contents

Preface

This book has been "in process" for over ten years. While preparing a creative service for the annual Sisterhood Sabbath at Temple Menorah of Redondo Beach, California, in March 1976, I looked up "Women" in several books of famous Jewish quotations. I read, "Engage not in too much conversation with women." "A woman will uncover a pot to see what her neighbor is cooking." "Let the law be burned rather than entrusted to a woman." These sayings were from the sages of our Talmud.

Of course, there were other quotations that honored women and exalted their position in the family, but my anger had been raised by the first ones, and I decided to use only the words of women in the text of the service I was preparing. This was easier said than done. Only a few of the standard anthologies of poetry and prayer included works by women. Using the limited resources available to me, I pulled together material from twenty women.

I was so moved by the women I "discovered"—Rosa Gutman-Jasny, Kadia Molodowsky, Nelly Sachs, Karen Gershon—that I thought it might be a good idea to find a few other poets and put out a small collection of women's poetry as a fund-raising project for the Sisterhood. I did my research at Hebrew Union College with the advice and support of Ariela Ehrlich and Harvey Horowitz, at the library of the Los Angeles Jewish Federation Council with the assistance of Morris Kaplan and Hava ben Zvi, by correspondence with Dr. Moshe Itzchaky of Bar Ilan University, and deep in the stacks at the University of Judaism.

During the search I consulted with a prominent male

scholar of bibliographies of Judaica. In an English translation of an early source book, Nahida Remy's *The Jewish Woman,* I gathered a list of women poets from the fourteenth to the eighteenth centuries. I wanted Mr. Scholar's help in finding their poems. He had been very animated at the prospect of helping me search for the lost poets until he saw my list. "But these are all women," he told me. "Their work would not have been preserved. Women are not good poets. The reason that they write poetry is that they aren't smart enough to write prose. In prose you need to know grammar and syntax. In poetry, if you don't know what to do, all you need is to put in a dash."

Spurred by his remarks, I became a feminist, determined to redeem the work of women through the ages. In addition to assistance from research libraries, I asked for help from my niece, Andrea Dworkin, who put me in touch with *Lilith Magazine* and many other women poets around the world. The network of women grew as word of my collection spread, until I now have poetry by over six hundred Jewish women.

The service that I created for Temple Menorah became my own Bat Mitzvah. In addition to writing the service, I chanted the Torah portion, and for the first time, at the age of forty-nine, I held the Torah in my arms. The hunt that I was conducting opened my eyes to the possibility of research on women's lives, and at fifty I enrolled in the School of Jewish Communal Service at Hebrew Union College/Jewish Institute of Religion.

In preparing the manuscript for an earlier unpublished anthology based on the collected material, I had typed over two hundred poems. Because poetry is a language of emotion, in the act of typing I took into myself the lives and feelings of Jewish women across time, so that when I finished the typing I felt again transformed. Since then I have been using this poetry to help other women get in touch with themselves and with the women who lived before us.

When it became clear that this was a bigger project than the Sisterhood could handle, I submitted it to trade and university publishers. One hundred fifty rejected the manuscript with best wishes and suggestions for other approaches. It seemed as if every major publisher had a Jewish woman poet as editor, who would send her own poems along with the rejection slip.

Irene Fine at the Women's Institute for Continuing Jewish Education in San Diego saw the possibility of publishing this book as part of its growing list of publications on women's spirituality. She created a *shidach* between myself and Debby Kremsdorf, and it has been our joy and pleasure to work together selecting, editing, and commenting on this collection.

Many women have helped along the way, and it would be impossible to name them all. Mahlia Lynn Schubert translated many of the poems from Yiddish to Hebrew. She also participated in the initial evaluation of poems for the anthology. Jenny Bornstein spent her last year reading, selecting, and translating many of the early Yiddish writers. When she had finished her last translation, she went to sleep and never awoke. (How I wish I had brought her another batch to translate; she might still be working away!) Women from the International Women's Writers Guild, Women Writers West, and the Creative Jewish Women's Alliance contributed poetry and support. Dr. Stanley Chyet of Hebrew Union College was an ongoing source of information and encouragement, as was Doris Gold of Biblio Press. Temple Bat Yam, Newport Beach, California, opened their library to us as a meeting place. The women of B'not Esh taught me to look at the language and women's perspective of God through new eyes and ears. Debbie Horowitz, Judith Rose, and Leora Zeitlin added their helpful insights. Betsy Arnold studied the prayers and aided in the final selection. Sharon Ann Jaeger helped in the final editing of the manuscript. Odile Barras, a French student of Literature, spent her summer in America sorting, filing, and checking on copyrights.

Since I first looked up "Women" in those collections of quotations, others have joined me in the search for women's past. There is now the Jewish Women's Resource Center at National Council of Jewish Women in New York. There are courses on Jewish women's studies in colleges and universities, collections, anthologies, bibliographies, scholarly and popular texts.

Above all, women have begun to search for their spiritual roots and an authentic language of prayer. They have come together to explore and share their past and present, while planning for the future. They are no longer silent, and as their voices join together, the whole of Judaism is changing.

Marcia Cohn Spiegel
Rolling Hills Estates, California
July, 1987

Introduction

Women have always needed spiritual expression, needed to pray. The earliest descriptions of Jewish women praising God occur in the Bible, in ceremonial expressions of joy. Miriam's song at the shores of the Red Sea, praising God with music and with dancing, is the first woman's prayer in Jewish history. In the *Book of Judges,* Jephthah's daughter came out singing, with timbrels and with dancing to welcome her father home. Again, in *First Samuel,* the women went out to greet Saul and David "with timbrels, with joy and with three-stringed instruments." These passages confirm that in biblical times there was a role in Jewish ritual for women.

Three more women's prayers appear in the Bible and the Apocrypha. The songs of Deborah and Judith both praise God for delivering the Israelites from their enemies. While Hannah's song also praises God, her story starts with a personal plea. Anxious and grieving because she was barren, she prayed for a child. Her frenzied and inarticulate behavior made the priest Eli believe she was drunk. When she explained her plight to him, he comforted and reassured her. After the birth of her son, Samuel, she composed her beautiful prayer of thanksgiving.

The prayers of our biblical foremothers have survived because they became an integral part of our oral tradition. Tragically, because many women were not literate, the feelings they expressed in prayer were never recorded or preserved. We are fortunate that even a few have been saved.

The purpose of this book is to present evidence of those prayers, to show the richness, strength, variety, and beauty of women's spiritual expression. Because there are still those who believe that spirituality in women is, at best, superficial and, at worst, dangerous, we hope this book will encourage modern women to reclaim their historic roles in Judaism.

EARLY HISTORY

A few prayers and poems have survived from the end of the biblical period until the sixteenth century. Writing materials were scarce and often perishable. Only a few relics remain to help us reconstruct the spiritual lives of women of this time.

In order to write, women have to be literate; they also need leisure, time free from the responsibilities of home and family. Since these elements are more accessible during a period of economic prosperity, it is not surprising that many of the prayers in this collection were written in eras when the economy was thriving.

During a period of upward mobility, a man could hire servants to free his wife and daughters from household work, thus his daughters could be educated. Their Jewish education, however, was probably limited to what was necessary to observe the laws of family purity and to run a Jewish home.

Eliazer ben Hyrcanus says in the Talmud, "It is better to burn the Torah than to teach it to your daughter." Although some rabbis disagreed with him, for many centuries the prevalent attitude was that girls were not to study Torah. Instead, they studied secular subjects, such as music, dancing, fine needlecrafts, and literature. While they studied the language of their native country, they did not study Hebrew. Few had any formal religious training.

Any woman who received a more extensive Jewish education generally was able to do so for a specific reason. Men like Rashi, who had no sons, taught their daughters. Clearly unmarriageable women were sometimes educated. Brilliant girls might be taught by their fathers, who did not consider the implications of this training for their daughters' future happiness.

One such woman was Rachel Morpurgo who lived in Italy in the middle of the nineteenth century. She was given an extensive education. When it came time for her to marry, she insisted on a love match and married someone who was not her intellectual equal. She had to support her family by sewing and could write her poetry only late at night.

Though much of the work in this anthology comes from wealthy women, the charming poem by Galah gives us a clue to another source—those who learned how to read and write because their families worked in the printing business. Prior to the Industrial Revolution, cottage industry prevailed. Most work was done at home, with adults and children all contributing. In the families of printers, women and children set type, and thus they had to be literate.

EXPANDING LITERACY

Movable type for the printing of Hebrew books developed in Venice. When the Venetian government ordered Jews to stop publishing their books in the late sixteenth century, Cracow and Prague became the next major centers of printing in Hebrew. Yiddish was a thriving language in Poland at that time, and since it is written with Hebrew letters, it was possible to use the same printing presses as for Hebrew to publish books in Yiddish and disseminate them cheaply.

Yiddish books for women also began to appear for the first time, mainly collections of prayers and Bible stories—some written by women. The *Tsena Urena* and collections of *Tehinot* are examples of books written in Yiddish for women. The *Tsena Urena* contained *midrashim* (commentaries), Bible stories, and explanations of prayers that could be used either in the synagogue or at home. The *Tehinot* are women's prayers.

Because more women had the opportunity to read and write, more literature from this period remains, and we had to be more selective in our editing. We have included several of these early selections so that the reader can get a feeling for women's lives and thoughts. *Written Out of History,* by Emily Taitz and Sondra Henry, published in 1983 by the Biblio Press in New York, is a good source for people interested in learning more about early Jewish women writers.

While there was no ritual role for women in public worship services, they did attend the synagogue, where behind the *mehitza* (barrier defining the women's section), there was frequently one woman, the *furzingeren,* who led the others in prayer. Deborah Ascarelli, a Jew from Rome, was possibly such a woman.

The sophisticated, lyrical poetry of Sarah Copia Sullam, writing in the Venetian ghetto, and of Deborah Ascarelli provides an interesting contrast to the simple dedication written in Yiddish by their contemporary, Roselle Fishels, from Crakow. By dedicating her *Shmuel* book—a collection of Psalms and stories of biblical heroes—to women and young girls, she showed her concern for their Jewish education and also proved that there existed a literate feminine audience.

When the Jews were expelled from Spain in the late fifteenth century, some established new communities in England and Holland. Among the descendants of these Sephardic Jews were Isabella Correa, Sara de Fonseca, and Isabel Henriques, seventeenth century poets who were praised by their contemporaries but whose work is lost to us.

MOVING TO MODERNITY

During the period of enlightenment in the mid-1800s, Jews who were striving toward the middle or upper class began educating their daughters to prepare them for participation in a changing society. The Socialist movement in eastern Europe originated during this period; later in the century the Zionist movement arose. Young people were looking beyond the religious education of the Yeshiva, toward the gymnasium and secular education. More women at all economic levels were educated.

By the start of the twentieth century, writing by women

was no longer limited only to periods of economic prosperity. Some of the best Yiddish writing was produced in New York, by secular Jews involved in the Socialist and Bundist Yiddish culture movements. It was a time of economic struggle, yet literacy rates were high.

Whether Hebrew or Yiddish, German or French, the language of prayer tells us in what language each poet was most fluent. The style is also revealing—early prayers in Yiddish were often very simple. By the late nineteenth and early twentieth centuries a more literate, sophisticated style had appeared. Alice Lucas' prayer shows the influence of her environment and to our ears it does not sound Jewish. The poetry of Else Lasker-Schuler and Nobel laureate Nelly Sachs reflects their high levels of education and acculturation.

How is God portrayed in a prayer? What does the woman say to God? What does she ask? How is her prayer influenced by the community and time in which she lives? The answers to these questions are clues that reveal, among other things, the writer's inner life, her sense of herself, and her degree of assimilation.

The earliest women's prayers praised God and God's power for victory. After the expulsion from Israel, when Jews lived in the Diaspora, the underlying questions persisted—"When will the Messiah come?" and "When will we return to Zion?" Later, after each terrible pogrom, women's writing suggests that the coming of the Messiah is imminent. Only after the Holocaust do angry poems begin to appear, poems that question God and God's relationship to the human race.

For almost fifteen years after the Holocaust, writers could not deal with its horrors or articulate their feelings about it. The flood of poems lamenting the Holocaust and questioning God's role in relationship to the Jewish people did not begin until the 1960s.

The sixties was also the era of hippies, the exploration of Eastern mystical religions, and the beginning of the women's movement. When these elements were juxtaposed, new avenues of expression arose. Writers looked for new ways to speak to God, new roles for God, a redefinition of God.

5

They struggled with God-language; the language that once had worked so comfortably no longer spoke for everyone. For some the obvious solution was to change all of the masculine gender words to feminine gender. Women rediscovered the Shechinah, the feminine aspect of God's imminence; but for some the problem remained because they perceived Shechinah as subsidiary to God, who is the Lord and Master. A feminine-gender God simply turned the "King" into a "Queen" and did not deal with the underlying theological issue of hierarchy.

In this book we have selected a historical sampling of Jewish women's prayers. We have included only one prayer by each poet, and we have tried to represent each of the periods for which we could find material. Because so many women are now writing prayers, it was difficult to choose from all the excellent contemporary material available. A great deal of fine work had to be omitted.

Since Jewish women are prominent among contemporary poets, in addition to the poets represented here, the reader may wish to refer to works by Muriel Rukeyser, Adrienne Rich, Robin Morgan, Erica Jong, Marge Piercy, Linda Pastan, Judith Viorst, Shirley Kaufman, and Eve Merriam.

Now the struggle is to find a language of prayer that is not exclusively feminine, a language that recognizes women as spiritual beings who have a need to pray and whose prayers may be different from men's prayers. There is a whole realm of prayers for women that have not yet been written—for women's roles, rituals, and life-cycle events.

Contemporary poets are exploring new images, new metaphors, and new forms of expression that are both more personal and more universal, and thus the end of the book is also a beginning.

Marcia Cohn Spiegel
Deborah Lipton Kremsdorf

Women Speak To God

*By presenting the prayers
chronologically we get a sense of
the evolution
of women's understanding
not only of God,
but also of themselves
and their roles.*

Two of the oldest poems attributed to women are simple songs from the Bible. On the occasion of a victory the women would greet their men with timbrels and with dancing.

The first of these was sung by Miriam when the pursuing Egyptian host had been drowned in the Red Sea.

———————————◆———————————

Sing to the Lord, for He has triumphed gloriously
Horse and driver He has hurled into the sea.
                    Exodus 15:20
                    Thirteenth century B.C.E.

After defeating the Philistines, Saul and David were praised by the women as they sang.

———————————◆———————————

Saul hath smitten his thousands,
And David his ten thousands.
                    Samuel 18:7
                    Thirteenth century B.C.E.

Excerpts from the Song of Deborah and Barak
Judges 5:3-31
Twelfth century B.C.E.

The Song of Deborah praises God for saving the Jews from the Canaanites. It was probably sung in alternate verses by Deborah and Barak.

———————————◆————————————

I, unto the Lord will I sing;
I will sing praise to the Lord, the God of Israel

       *   *   *

Awake, awake, Deborah;
Awake, awake utter a song;
Arise, Barak, and lead thy captivity captive, thou son of
      Abinoam.

       *   *   *

Blessed above women shall Jael be,
The wife of Heber the Kenite,
Above women in the tent shall she be blessed.
Water he asked, milk she gave him;
In a lordly bowl she brought him curd.
Her hand she put to the tent pin,
And her right hand to the workmen's hammer;
And with the hammer she smote Sisera, she smote
      through his head,
Yea, she pierced and struck through his temples.
At her feet he sunk, he fell, he lay;
At her feet he sunk, he fell;
Where he sunk, there he fell down dead.

Through the window she looked forth, and peered.
The mother of Sisera, through the lattice:
'Why is his chariot so long in coming?
Why tarry the wheels of his chariots?'

       *   *   *

So perish all Thine enemies, O Lord;

But they that love Him be as the sun when he goeth
　　forth in his might.
And the land had rest forty years.

Excerpts from Hannah's Prayer
I Samuel 2:1-10
Eleventh century B.C.E.

Hannah sang her joyous prayer of thanksgiving after the birth of her son, Samuel. Some have conjectured that the word "horn" may refer to the womb.

———————————

My heart exalteth in the Lord,
My horn is exalted in the Lord;
My mouth is enlarged over mine enemies;
Because I rejoice in Thy salvation.
There is none holy as the Lord;
For there is none beside Thee;
Neither is there any rock like our God.

Multiply not exceeding proud talk;
Let not arrogancy come out of your mouth;
For the Lord is a God of knowledge,
And by Him actions are weighed.
The bows of the mighty men are broken,
And they that stumbled are girded with strength,
They that were full have hired out themselves for bread;
And they that were hungry have ceased;
While the barren hath borne seven,
She that had many children hath languished.

The Lord killeth, and maketh alive;
He bringeth down to the brave, and bringeth up.
The Lord maketh poor, and maketh rich;
He bringeth low and lifteth up.
He raiseth up the poor out of the dust,
He lifteth up the needy from the dung hill,
To make them sit with princes,
And inherit the throne of glory;
For the pillars of the earth are the Lord's,
And he hath set the world upon them.

He will keep the feet of His holy ones,
But the wicked shall be put to silence in darkness;
For not by strength shall man prevail.
They that strive with the Lord shall be broken to pieces;
Against them will He thunder in heaven;
The Lord will judge the ends of the earth;
And He will give strength unto His king,
And exalt the horn of His anointed.

Excerpts from Judith's Song of Thanksgiving
Book of Judith 16:2-17
352 B.C.E.

Judith's song in the Apocrypha not only acknowledges God's power and judgment, but as the following excerpts bear witness also demonstrates that women can serve Judiasm heroically.

———————————◆———————————

Begin unto my God with timbrels,
Sing unto my Lord with cymbals;
Tune unto him psalm and praise;
Exalt him and call upon his name.

*   *   *

The Almighty Lord brought them to naught by the hand
    of a woman.
For their mighty one did not fall by young men,
Neither did sons of Titans smite him,
Nor did high giants set upon him:
But Judith the daughter of Merari made him weak with
    the beauty of her countenance.

*   *   *

I will sing unto my God a new song:
O Lord, thou art great and glorious,
Marvelous in strength, invincible.
Let all thy creation serve Thee:
For thou spakest, and they were made,
Thou didst send forth thy spirit, and it builded there,
And there is none that shall resist thy voice,
For the mountains shall be moved from their
    foundations with the waters,
And the rock shall melt as wax at thy presence:
But thou art yet merciful to them that fear Thee.
For all sacrifice is little for a sweet savour.
And all the fat is very little for a whole burnt offering
    to Thee:

But he that feareth the Lord is great continually.

*   *   *

Woe to the nation that rise up against my race:
The Lord Almighty will take vengeance of them in the
  day of judgment,
To put fire and worms in their flesh;
And they shall weep and feel their pain for ever.

There is a City
Sambetha — "The Jewish Sibyl"
Second century B.C.E.
Translated from the Greek by Bohn

Sambetha (or Sabbe) was a Jewish Sybilline oracle. Using
the Oracle's standard poetic form, she proselytized the Greek-
speaking, Hellenistic Jews back to their own religious values.

———————————◆———————————

There is a city Chaldean Ur
Whence come the race of most upright men,
Who are ever right-minded and their works good.
They are neither concerned for the sun's course,
Nor the moon's, nor for monstrosities on earth,
Nor for satisfaction from ocean's depths,
Nor for signs of sneezing and the augury from birds;
Nor for soothsaying, nor sorcery, nor incantations,
Nor for deceitful follies of ventriloquists.

They do not, Chaldean fashion, astrologize,
Nor watch the stars...
But they are concerned about rightness and virtue.
Their measures are just both in field and in city.
They do not steal from each other by night,
Nor drive off herds of oxen and sheep and goats.
Nor does neighbor remove his neighbor's landmarks.
Nor does the wealthy vex the poor one,
Nor oppress widows, but such rather assists them,
Providing them always with grain, wine and oil;
Always a blessing to those in want among them.
He gives back part of His harvest to the needy people,
For "The Heavenly" made the earth common to all.

With the Help of God
Roselle Fishels
1586, Poland
Translated from the Yiddish by Mahlia Lynn Schubert

This simple poem was written as the dedication to a popular retelling of biblical hero stories, the *Shmuel Book*. The translator has retained both the rhythm and the style of the original. Note the contrast with the more complex poetry of Fishels' contemporaries, Sarah Copia Sullam and Deborah Ascarelli.

With the help of God, blessed be His name,
With the help of God, I will endure the same.

In time, the holy psalms will prove to all
That Jews who praise God will never fall,

These psalms, whether by woman or man begun,
And, as King David, blessed be he, had done.

I never discouraged, and where I did go,
Taught to all who wanted to know;

Until they began to come, one and all, to me.
I also gave psalms to Moshe Vondri,

Here, to the holy city of Hanover, the psalms I
    donated:
At the same time, by Rav Moshe Standl they were
    translated.

Now songs from the book of Samuel could be sung
By all as well in our own mother tongue,

And reading them, easier and pleasant to do,
For men and women and young girls, too.

My Inmost Hope
Sarah Copia Sullam
1590, Venice
Translated from the Italian

Sara Copia Sullam (1592-1641) was hostess to the leading
Jewish and non-Jewish intellectuals of her community in
Venice. Her correspondence with the Genoese monk, Ansaldo
Ceba, was discovered after his death. She subsequently was
accused of heresy, and although she successfully defended
herself against the charges, this prayer indicates she may never
have felt free of the taint of these charges.

O Lord, you know my inmost hope and thought,
You know whene'er before your Judgment's throne
I shed salt tears and uttered many a moan,
'Twas not for vanities that I besought.
O turn on me your look with mercy fraught,
And see how envious malice makes me groan!
The pall upon my heart by error thrown
Remove; illumine me with your radiant thought.
At truth let not the wicked scorner mock.
O you who breathes in me a spark divine
The lying tongue's deceit with silence blight,
Protect me from its venom, you, my Rock,
And show the spiteful sland'rer by this sign
That you will shield me with your endless night.

Prayer
Deborah Ascarelli
Sixteenth century, Venice
Translated from the Hebrew by Avshalom Cohen

Deborah Ascarelli may have led the women's prayers in
the Ascarelli family synagogue in Rome. Her translations
from Hebrew to Italian and Italian to Hebrew are said to
be the first work published by a Jewish woman.

––––––––––––––•––––––––––––––

"And God created man in His image.
In the image of God He created him."
And He made him a little lower than God
And honor and glory is His crown—
For whether you have dignity or not
Sin is at your door
And your desires will be ruled by you alone.
The heavens tell of the greatness of God
And the marvels of His work.

He is your glory
And He is your God, who made you
And the marvels that your eyes have seen,
"These people I formed for myself
And they will tell of my glory."

Prayer
Galah
1718, Minsk
Translated from the Yiddish by Bertha Held
and Mahlia Lynn Schubert

This charming poem gives us insight into the life of a young Jewish maiden. Since there is no way of indicating a capital letter in Yiddish, the translators wondered whether "my father's house" should have read "my Father's house." Galah was literate probably because she worked in her family's printing business.

————————————•————————————

This pretty new prayer, from beginning to end,
I arranged, with all the letters in my own hand.

I, Galah, daughter of Moshe the printer
And my mother, Freda, daughter of Israel Katz,
Blessed be his memory.

And Freda gave birth to me among ten children;
I am a virgin, and almost twelve years old.

It should not surprise you that I must work,
The soft and delicate daughter of Israel
　　　has long been in exile.

One year goes out and the next comes in,
And still we have not experienced our Savior.

We shout and beg God all year long,
When will our prayers finally come before God?

In the meantime I must be silent,
In my father's house one must not say much;

Whatever happens to Israel
Our own destiny will reveal,

And, as the sacred book says,
Someday all will be freed from destruction,
All who have wept out of Zion.

Prayer Before Sleep
Alice Lucas
Late 1850s, England

There is a quality to this poem reminiscent of the English children's bedtime prayer, "Now I Lay Me Down to Sleep." It is a good illustration of the way that women's writing reflects the environment in which they live. Alice Lucas' translations of medieval Jewish poetry were included in English prayerbooks of the nineteenth century.

Bless'd art Thou, O Lord of all,
Who mak'st the bands of sleep to fall
Upon mine eyes, and slumber press
Mine eyelids down with heaviness.

God of my fathers, may it be
Thy will, this night to suffer me
To lay me down in peace and rise
In peace, when morning gilds the skies.

From thoughts of ill my slumber keep
And, lest the sleep of death I sleep,
O lighten Thou mine eyes, for Thou,
Lord, dost with light the eye endow.

Bless'd art Thou, O Lord most high,
Who in Thy glorious majesty
And in Thy gracious love hast given
Light upon earth and light in heaven.

Then We'll Be Privileged
Rachel Morpurgo
1855, Trieste
Translated from the Hebrew by Elisa Blankstein

Having received a fine education from her prominent
Italian family, Rachel Morpurgo married against their wishes.
In her eighty-two years she produced a large body of work
in Hebrew. This joyous paean captures the spirit of the hymns
of Miriam, Deborah and Judith.

We'll be privileged to go out
Chanting and dancing
To sing with a voice so pleasing,
To the Good Shepherd.

The mountains and hills
Will break forth in song.
The tree leaves will clap
Their hands.

To give thanks unto the Lord
In the Temple Ariel
Then the entire nation will see!

Into Zion comes a Savior
The salvation of Israel.
And in their lead, Hananel.

Excerpts from "I Never Loved a Flower"
Grace Aguilar
1873, England

Descended from a prominent Spanish family who fled to
England during the Inquisition, Grace Aguilar published eight
books and many poems in her thirty-one years. Her book
Women in Israel was a feminist examination of the traditional
Jewish woman's role. This poem may reflect her years of
illness and confinement.

I never loved a flower,
    And cherish'd it with pride,
But it wither'd in its home of love,
    And bow'd its head and died.

      *   *   *

I never loved a friend,
    But parting's fiat came,
And sympathies were sever'd that
    Ne'er seem'd again the same.

I never felt deep gladness,
    But a silent shadow stole,
E'en 'mid the laughing flowers that twined
    A moment o'er my soul.

      *   *   *

Oh, come back to thy stillness,
    And dwell there with thy God;
His blessed paths of quietness
    Securely thou has trod.

And though no dazzling flowers
    May there breathe tales of glee,
And mirth's light laugh no echo finds:
    In safety thou wilt be.

Our Father's smile will lead thee,

His love will go before—
Return! return, my spirit—Oh,
   Come to thy God once more.

Prayer on the Approach of Accouchement
Fanny Neuda
1878, Vienna

The *tehinot* or personal prayers for women written by
Fanny Neuda touched every facet of women's lives in the
nineteenth century. Her poignant prayers, such as those for
a child moving to a foreign land or for a husband who is
traveling far from home, reveal the uncertainties and fears
that were a part of a woman's existence.

O my God! More and more it approaches the great hour,
On which I shall give birth to another being,
According to Thy wise ordination. O God!
Thou knowest my weakness, Thou will pardon me
That I look toward that hour with dread and anxiety.
For Thou, Omniscient One, alone knowest
What that hour shall be unto me.
Therefore I call unto Thee, from the depths of my soul.
Fortify me with strength and courage in the hour of danger,
God of Mercy! Grant that the life of my child may not
    be my death!
Shorten the woes and pains that await me,
Let Thy help be nigh unto me in the moment of danger,
And do not remember the multitude of my sins.
Convert, O God! my pain into delight
At the lovely sight of a living, well-formed and healthful
    babe,
Whose heart may ever be dedicated unto Thee.
Lord! Have mercy upon me!
Into Thy hand I confide my life,
Keep and preserve me from all evil.
                Amen.

Poems by Abbie Hatch and Minnie Louis appeared in the
first periodical specifically for Jewish women, *The American
Jewess,* published in Chicago by Rose Sonnenschein. Minnie
Louis' alliterative acrostic is patterned after ancient *piyutim.*

All Right in the End
Abbie Hatch
1889, United States

Your heart is bowed with a transient grief,
    Your eyes are misty with tears;
There is sorrow deep and there's no relief
    Ahead in the maze of years.
So it seems to you as you weep to-day,
    Yet sorrow may be your friend;
So keep up your courage awhile and pray,
    'Twill come out right in the end.

There never was day so dark and drear
    But what, ere the sands had run,
The clouds would shift and the heavens clear
    To the smiling face of the sun.
There never was cruel stab or blow
    Inflicted by foe or friend,
But there was a balm—He willed it so—
    'Twill come out right in the end.

Psalms
Minnie D. Louis
1896, United States

Psalms profound in prayer and praise,
Softly soothe the soul that strays.
Abject aft th' Almighty's arc;
Lord lent lyrics, like the lark,
Mount in melody; mind's new morn,
Sun-lit spreads of shadows shorn.

Passionate Sword
Jean Starr Untermeyer
1921, United States

Although Jean Starr Untermeyer's large body of work was
written for a general audience, a number of her poems
demonstrate the spiritual concerns of a Jewish woman.

Temper my spirit, O Lord,
Burn out its alloy,
And make it a pliant steel for thy welding,
Not a clumsy toy,
A blunt, iron thing in my hands
That blunder and destroy.

Temper my spirit, O Lord,
Keep it long in the fire;
Make it one with the flame. Let it share
That up-reaching desire.
Grasp it thyself, O my God,
Swing it straighter and higher!

To God

Else Lasker-Schüler
Circa 1920, Germany
Translated from the German by Audri Durchslag
and Jeanette Litman-Demeestere

Else Lasker-Schuler, one of the most prominent poets of
the early twentieth century, led a bohemian life in Berlin.
Poems written during the turmoil of pre-war Germany
display her strong Jewish identity. Her books were burned
by the Nazis.

———————————•———————————

You do not hinder the good and the evil stars;
All their moods stream forth.
In my brow a furrow throbs,
A deep crown with dusky light.

But my world is still—
You never hindered my mood.
God, where are You?

I'd want to listen closely at Your heart,
In Your most distant nearness to find my counterpart,
If, from Your kingdom's endlessly blessed light,
Goldenly transformed,
All the good and the evil fountains rush.

The Maabaroth
Rikudah Potash
Circa 1925, Israel
Translated from the Yiddish by Joseph Leftwich

Rikudah Potash, born in Poland, moved to Palestine in her late teens. This translation of her Yiddish poem describes the Zionists' first primitive settlements and the people's yearning to have a better life in Israel.

Good evening, Lord God,
I have a prayer to you,
Lord God,
For our Maabaroth.

It is not enough
That our people come
From horror and from blood,
It is not enough that they come to us,
To live in Maabaroth.
It is not enough, Lord God!

Their Ark is smaller than Noah's Ark.
And no dove comes to their door.
What comes is the rain beating down on their roofs,
Beating down in a steady pour.

What comes is the wind, cold as ice,
Biting into their bones.
In all the Maabaroth, Lord God,
You hear children's cries and old people's groans.

Give them strong roofs and walls, Lord God,
And windows to let in light,
Shield them from the wind and rain,
Give them comfort in the night.

Good evening, Lord God,
I have a prayer to You,
Lord God,
For our Maabaroth.

I Know Not Your Way
Malka Heifetz Tussman
1949, United States
Translated from the Yiddish by Marcia Falk

A prominent Yiddish poet, Malka Heifetz Tussman came
to the United States in 1912. She resided in Berkeley,
California, where she wrote her lyrical poetry in Yiddish.

I know not your ways—
A sunset is for me
a Godset.
Where are you going,
God?
Take me along,
if, in the "along,"
it is light,
God.

I am afraid of the dark.

In Your Image
Shulamis Yelin
1975, Montreal

Shulamis Yelin's poetry grows out of her experiences as a Canadian Jewish woman. She frequently writes about her search for spirituality.

———————————◆———————————

In your image,
in your image, God,
You made me in your image,
and I reach upward, seeking—
to be like You, God.

Just? Like You I'm vengeful.
Merciful? Like You I seek an understanding heart.
Jealous? Yes, I'm jealous
and iniquitous
and long suffering—
and like You
I dream to make a world,
(in miniature, God),
to do my bidding.

And loving I can be, yes, loving,
to a penitent punished child.

Yet clearly, God, most clearly,
do I see in me your oneness,
your all-oneness,
your aloneness—
in my heart.

How Long Have We Forgotten How to Listen
Nelly Sachs
1967, Sweden

Nobel laureate Nelly Sachs is known as the poet of the Holocaust. Although she fled Berlin to the safety of Sweden, she continued to write about the horror of the death camps.

"Before they spring forth I tell you of them"
Isaiah 42:9

How long have we forgotten how to listen!
He planted us once to listen
Planted us like lyme grass by the eternal sea,
We wanted to grow on fat pastures,
To stand like lettuce in the kitchen garden.

Although we have business
That leads us far
From His light,
Although we drink tap water,
And only as it dies it reaches
Our eternally thirsting mouths—
Although we walk down a street
Beneath which earth has been silenced
By a pavement,
We must not sell our ears,
Oh, we must not sell our ears.
Even in the market,
In the computation of dust,
Many had made a quick leap
Onto the tightrope of longing,
Because they heard something,
And leapt out of the dust
And sated their ears.
Press, oh press on the day of destruction
The listening ear to the earth,

And you will hear, through your sleep
You will hear
How in death
Life begins.

Sabbath

As the keystone
of the Jewish religion,
Sabbath observance is central
to Jewish identity.
The wide range of feelings
for the Sabbath
echoes the diversity
of Jewish cultural
experiences.

Prayer for Sabbath
Chana Katz
1817, Holland
Translated from the Yiddish by Bertha Held
and Mahlia Lynn Schubert

In the early nineteenth century Chana Katz described, in
simple rhymed couplets, the joys of the Sabbath and her faith
that Sabbath observance would lead to the coming of the
Messiah.

Dear God I sing my praise to You,
Creator of all things, old and new

And gratefully we all give thanks
That You made us Your chosen people.

How proud we are, our God is You,
Creator of heaven, the earth we view.

Good food, sweet drink from which we live
With all the pleasures and joys You give.

And whoever the beloved Sabbath keeps pure,
Will be deserving of husband and children,
Respect and riches will come to her.

So I keep holy Sabbath with its obligations,
With all the good food, the sweets and the spices,
And what is prepared, let it be what entices.

This dear holy Sabbath, like a Garden of Eden,
Let us please deserve it also in heaven.

And Beloved Messiah shall lead us by the right hand,
And bring us into that holy land.

Daughters of Israel
Peninah Moise
1841, United States

Charleston, South Carolina, is justly proud of Peninah
Moise, who composed the first American Jewish hymnal.
Some of the poems in it can still be found in Reform Jewish
prayerbooks.

———————————— • ————————————

Daughters of Israel, arise!
    The Sabbath-morn to greet,
Send songs and praises to the skies
    Then frankincense more sweet.

Take heed, lest ye the drift mistake
    Of heaven's hallowed hours,
And from those dreams too late awake,
    That show you but life's flowers.

Leave not the spirit unarrayed,
    To deck the mortal frame;
With gems of grace let woman aid
    Charms that from nature came.

With jewels of a gentle mind,
    More precious far than gold,
Brightened by love, by faith refined,
    And set in chastest mould.

Wife! mother! sister! on ye all
    A tender task devolves;
Child, husband, brother, on ye call
    To nerve the best resolves.

Your hands must gird the buckler on,
    The moral weapons cleanse,
By which that battle may be won,
    That in self-conquest ends.

Sabbath Eve
Jessie Sampter
1937, United States and Israel

Influenced by Henrietta Szold, Jessie Sampter left the comforts of the United States to pioneer in Palestine, where she taught Yemenite Jews and published two fine books of verse.

———————————◆———————————

Sarah, the Princess, in her door
Stands basking in the lowered sun;
The Sabbath light is on her face
Of many labors done.

Her brow is lined with graven lines,
A kerchief whitely round it tied;
Mother of mothers, tall and strong,
Broad-hipped and tender-eyed!

The tenements that teem with youth
Resound with children of her kin;
But she stands silent, Sabbath-eyed,
Her quiet soul within.

Her sons are like the rocks of earth,
So strong and terrible and mild,
Because she taught them ancient prayers
Too fearful for a child.

Friday Night
Karen Gershon
1966, England

Born in Germany, Karen Gershon escaped to England
before the outbreak of World War II. She writes about the
impact of the War on herself, her family and the community
from which she fled.

———————————•———————————

I would have joined the Jews of my home town in
    prayer
not to praise God but to make myself feel I belonged
in my hallowed childhood servitude I was freer
I am shackled by what I have lost to all that has
    changed

When choir and congregation answered the cantor
my voice was inaudible under the organ-notes
but I was Ruth I was Esther I was at the centre
where the synagogue stood are now offices and flats

To join in traditional singing was all I wanted
to pause for a moment as if I had really come home
I should have suspected the price of what I was granted
without persecution God is not the same

Despite their assimilation into the American experience, Charlotte Anker, Brenda Gevertz, Florence Victor, and Diane Levenberg all express their strong connections to their Jewish roots.

The Sabbath
Charlotte Anker
1966, United States

What do I
Whose child eyes glowed with envy at the sight
Of fir trees strung with Christmas light
Know of the Sabbath?

What can I
Who smiled on springtime's gayer rites and petulantly said:
"Why must we eat unleavened bread?"
Say of the Sabbath?

How should I
Who, rebel-masked, scorned Friday evening's candle
      glow and outstretched hands
And asked, "Why can't we simply be Americans?"
Observe the Sabbath?

Yet, through some process science still endeavors to define,
One day I looked on four millennia carved by chance or
      some design
And said, "All this is mine."

When oven smoke curled black above Auschwitz,
      Dachau, Belsen
And ashes, soap, gold teeth amassed where once a
      people, learned, proud, had been,
I felt the numbers burn into my skin.

When shtetl artisans and scholars watched their
      neighbors murder, loot, harass

And re-avowed their faith and blessed the wine and
    said, "This, too, shall pass."
I drained a glass.

When ships sailed from Spain laden with the seed of
    Jews who had, for centuries, Iberian rule endured,
And oceans deepened with the tears of that vast horde,
I stood on board.

The wails of prophets, brilliance of the kings, with all
    their flaws,
The mettle of the men who gave the Romans pause,
Grasped me with vise-like claws.

At last, I stood with Moses on the mountain, heard
    God's will expressed.
And when He said, "On this day ye shall rest,"
I was impressed.

Suburban Shabbes
Brenda Gevertz
1974, United States

Shabbes was served.
On flannel-backed white vinyl from a Goodman's mix,
    Manischewitz can and with a little help from the
    deli at the mall.
The kiddush was short. There was no ornate silver cup
    filled beyond the brim, no embroidered yamulkas
    or decorated challah cover.
There was challah.
In pre-cut perfect slices it shared the bread basket along
    with seedless rye.

The challah, squashed in the car ride home, looked
    deformed next to the uniform arcs of rye. It should
    have been covered.
The horseradish did not bring tears.
We did not sing zemiros, but the phone rang and the
    coffee perked a 20th-century symphony
    accompanied by crashing ice cubes in the yellow
    Frigidaire.
It was not the horseradish but the thousands of years of
    lost culture that made the eyes tear.

Friday Night Cantata
(While Listening to Bach's Cantata No. 51)
Florence Victor
1957, New York

Unfit for worship, still I learned each prayer,
And hoping that the rabbi couldn't tell
It was the music which I loved so well,
And not his God, and not his patent stare
Which broke the spell, I shook hands in despair
And fled the synagogue, an infidel
Who craved only a song, who feared no hell
But speech or silence, sanctity left bare.

My heresy full-grown, I often now
Stand waif-like while the congregation prays;
Idolater of sound, I must profane
The joy in God each offering displays,
And yet alone on Friday night I bow
To something even Bach could not explain.

Friday Night
Diane Levenberg
1976, New York

They had something those Jews
who went out to take in
their double portion a day
of rest beginning with a
Friday night gift I've
long since exchanged

Just before sunset it begins to
hurt and each week a homesickness for
a different kind of home begins
and I choose again and again
to try and ignore it

Friday night meant sitting
with my young father and mother
by the light of the candles all
of us very quiet and even then
I wanted to know if I could break
through the walls of my grapefruit
both of them laughing gently at
a child they loved

Friday night then and now is
Russian music challah crumbs
in the pages of a *Jewish Folklore*
A cello concerto in minor
lighted candles in the kitchen
a dim bulb in the bathroom
and one soft reading light near
the living room couch and I
try to escape this 5,000 year old
tradition in a grimy bar
the only connection to my Friday night
is that I'm still drinking wine.

Kabbalat Shabbat
Sandy Eisenberg Sasso
1974, Philadelphia

Rabbi Sandy Eisenberg Sasso is one of the first women ordained in the United States. Her poem reflects a growing complexity and conflict in Jewish women's spiritual expression.

Descend
> Descend deep
>> Into ancient ancestral cave
>> Candles' flame
>>> Blessed by muted, whispered prayer
>>>> lights our way

Descend
> Descend deeper
>> Into the time-honored womb
>> of sweat and blood
>> But do not touch
>>> the walls of hallowed stone

Find there
> half virgin bride
>> half whoring demoness
>>> she who offers twisted sacrificial breads

Gaze upward—for relief—
> as candle's flames point
>> to airy field
>>> where those rejoicing
>>> through song
>>>> dance and
>>>> reverberating prayer

> Welcome a fictitious Sabbath bride

Light A Candle
Zelda
1967, Israel
Translated from the Hebrew by Marcia Falk

Although a traditionally observant Jewish woman, Zelda's
poetry has wide popularity in Israel among both secular and
religious Jews.

———————————◆———————————

Light a candle.
Drink wine.
Softly the Sabbath has plucked
the sinking sun.
Slowly the Sabbath descends,
the rose of heaven in her hand.

How can the Sabbath
plant a huge and shining flower
in a blind and narrow heart?
How can the Sabbath
plant the bud of angels
in a heart of raving flesh?
Can the rose of eternity grow
in an age enslaved
to destruction,
an age enslaved
to death?

Light a candle!
Drink wine!
Slowly the Sabbath descends
and in her hand
the flower,
and in her hand
the sinking sun.

Shechinah
Chana Bell
1977, Los Angeles

Chana Bell introduces the image of the *Shechinah,* the feminine aspect of God, in her poem of welcome to the Sabbath, which parallels Chana Katz' description of the joy and peace of the day of rest.

———————————•———————————

Perched on our shoulders
a colorful butterfly
you whisper
into pores
shabbat's sweetness

we breathe you in
breathe the week out
take in roundness
letting go of sharp angles

we breathe in the *neshama yiteira*
the soul of the world to come
in awe
we sway   not march

As we kindle shabbat candles
you glide into our dark corners
warming us
dissolving our dense bodies
into light

Questions, Rebellion and Reconciliation

*In a world in which
they have no control or power
over the events of life,
women cry out to God in anger,
struggling to come to terms
with events that are beyond
comprehension.*

If God Had Known
Hortense Flexner
1919, United States

This poem appeared in the *Menorah Journal,* which
published outstanding Jewish scholars, writers and poets.

━━━━━━━━━◆━━━━━━━━━

If God had known,
In the long, starless night,
Before the first dawn shed
Its gleam on cloud and wave in chaos rolled;
That one—a child—an instant's winged gold,
Should for her body's hunger thus be sold;
O would He then have said,
"Let There Be Light"!

If He had known,
When in the seething murk
He bound the waters wild,
And hung the skies before Him for a veil,
Two souls should yearn and catch a glimpse and fail,
Wait in the gray till passion had grown stale,
O, would He then have smiled
Upon His work?

Disquisition
Chana Bloch
1967, Oakland, California

In order to protect the sanctity of God's name, traditional
Jews write G-D. Chana Bloch (a professor at Mills college)
uses humor to challenge this custom.

———————————•———————————

One day I dared to put the O back
in G-d.
I watched Him bulge to God—
  paunchy, respectable
and sad.

I brooded about my heresy
until I guessed
that God who loves the circle best
  only to find
  our angularity
might after all not mind.

   He'd take it to heart, perhaps,
   if I chose to drop the caps.

But O that fine round O
  fleshed out from the scrawny spine
  of a minus sign—
  or would He object that O
  was zero,
  taking Him in vain?

God knows,
an O is an O is an O,
  and slyly checks
  our tic-tac-toe
with His wry X.

Questions
Bea Stadtler
1965, United States

Early poets primarily praised God's power, but in moments
of personal sorrow many contemporary poets question God.

Oh God,
if there is a God,
How have I visualized You?
What image have I made of You?
For here I sit, silently talking to You
And next to me sits her mother,
the mother of my friend
who was named the same as I.
Elohim—God of justice
when the *Sefer Ha-Chayim* was closed
at *Ne-ilah* on Yom Kippur
why oh why
was my name written for life
and hers for death?
I looked at her mother's tears
and I wondered,
for she was good and kind
and she had children to live for.
Why then was I chosen to live
and she to die?

All I find is the echo in my heart
an imponderable question:
Why?

God of Mercy
Kadia Molodowsky
1945, New York
Translated from the Yiddish by Irving Howe

The terror of the Holocaust moved the poet to confront
God's justice. Kadia Molodowsky was one of the most
prominent Yiddish poets of the early twentieth century.

O God of Mercy
For the time being
Choose another people.
We are tired of death, tired of corpses,
We have no more prayers.
For the time being
Choose another people.
We have run out of blood
For victims,
Our houses have been turned into deserts,
The earth lacks space for tombstones,
There are no more lamentations
Nor songs of woe
In the ancient texts.

God of Mercy
Sanctify another land
Another Sinai.
We have covered every field and stone
With ashes and holiness.
With our crones
With our young
With our infants
We have paid for each letter in your Commandments.

God of Mercy
Lift up your fiery brow,
Look on the peoples of the world,
Let them have the prophecies and Holy Days

Who mumble your words on every tongue.
Teach them the Deeds
And the ways of temptation.

God of Mercy
Give to us rough clothing
Of shepherds who tend sheep
Of blacksmiths at the hammer
Of washerwomen, cattle slaughterers
And lower still.
And O God of Mercy
Grant us one more blessing—
Take back the gift of our separateness.

If

Rose Gutman-Jasny
1939, United States
Translated from the Yiddish by Etta Blum

The poet pits women's power to give birth against God's power to destroy. It is a challenge that only women can issue.

If another flood should come,
Let us, sisters all, from every land,
Say to God in his looming tower:

Whom are you hitting? Would you smite grasses
For their grassy sins? For the crooked paths
And dark tangles to which you destined them?
For their scanty roots which push toward earth,
Remote from your face?

If another flood should come,
We will take a dark view of it.
Let us, sisters all, from every land,
Say to God:
Turn back your punishing hand!

As a ravaged field cannot nourish seed,
So our deprived bodies will be sealed.
You'll conduct the Sabbath for desert winds
And smite the sea with thunder for its sins.

Sinai

Joanne Seltzer

1983, Schenectady, New York

The poem objects to the ancient covenant between God
and the Jewish people.

———————————•———————————

Because you once brought me out of Egypt
you expect me to serve you forever
and let bygones be bygones. I object
to the deal Moses made. Having been there
when you spoke, I remember how Moses
said you were O.K. And I remember
the idols I used to invoke: losses
like that demand some kind of payback. Where
were you, Omnipotent One, when people
cried out to you on the stake? Does the char
of human flesh excite your sense of smell?
Or do you lean more toward the odor
of a death camp? God, will you punish me
for asking what you've done for me lately?

Faith and Reason
Lillian Ott
1949, Chicago

Lillian Ott continues the convenantal theme.

Somewhere in this teasing, tantalizing universe
    among the hurtling planets
or past the celestial infinities of shadeless dark,
God and man must meet;

Whether in the sealed cell of the conscience,
in the imagery of sight or in sensing,
or beyond conscious knowledge and feeling,
a time must come when Creator and creation need audit
    accounts
and make amends for sins mutually committed
in each other's name.

Kol Nidre
(For an Adolescent During the Holocaust)
Rosa Felsenburg Kaplan
1982, Los Angeles

The Kol Nidre prayer, which ushers in the day of atonement, annuls unfulfillable vows that Jews have made to God. In her parallel prayer, Rosa Felsenburg Kaplan acknowledges the pain of a survivor in her search for peace.

All the vows
And all the promises not kept
Because life was too short
Or too difficult,
Or we were too young,
Not wise enough, or too weak—
Let them be cancelled!

I remember being glad
To leave behind my friend and Europe.
When she told me how life was started,
She had sworn me to secrecy.
Now she would not have to know
That I had told our secret.

The choking void of unsaid farewells
Because we did not know
We were together for the last time—
Let it be closed!

Alice and Malka, twin cousins with whom I played,
And who I wished I looked like,
And whose parents, I thought,
Must love them more than mine loved me—
"One time," said their mother, "They mostly took
        young girls..."

For the sins committed on them
Forgive us: *S'lach lanu, m'chal lanu, kape lanu!*

61

The unsaid thanks
To those who gave to us,
Life, sometimes,
But to whom we could not give—
Let thanks be understood!

Twice I took another's name
To cross a border
What happened to my namesakes?

And to Onkel Michel,
And Tante Esti
And Kati Neni—
Who took me in, housed me and fed me,
And whom I loathed and made fun of
Because they were not my parents,
Nor like them...?

The tears unshed
Because we were too busy living
To mourn—
Let them now flow!

Trying to finish high school
And enter college,
Becoming American—
I shut my eyes to my parents' fears,
My heart to their losses as well as to my own...

To those of us who live,
To our families and friends,
And all of those whom we're supposed to love—
Father of mercy,
Give them life
And us, time enough
To make peace,
Perhaps even to love them.

Once God Commmanded Us
Leah Goldberg
1948, Israel
Translated from the Hebrew by Ramah Commanday

One of the foremost Hebrew poets of Israel, Leah
Goldberg, finds courage to continue as a Jew.

Once God commanded us to stand firm
under His terrible Tree of Life.
And we stood, beaten by hope in the black, windy years.
Perhaps the fruit would fall at our feet?
But nothing happened.

And when the day arrived
when we secretly
added our scores with God,
We saw the cowering landscape,
the brown, fallen leaves.
And the wind still blows against our faces.
Then the Divine echo said,
"This is the day of your freedom.
This is all. It is good."

I will walk alone on the edge of a blade,
just a few steps
toward the same flickering lamp
on the corner of the street.

In a New Voice

*The poems in this section
represent a process of
creating new images,
metaphors and prayer.
They are the leading edge
of the movement for more
universal spiritual
expression.*

Genesis
Ruth Brin
1964, Minneapolis

Ruth Brin incorporates the simplicity of the original story
of Genesis and the complexity of modern science to present
the act of creation in the metaphor of birth.

In the beginning, You made a simple world,
day and night, water and earth, plants and animals

But now You create galaxies beyond systems
in the unending curve of space

Now we know You create with subtlety
the invisible atom with its secret heart of power

You create with delicacy, with violence,
the cell, splitting, becoming life

Filled with joy, You make a human being
a whole world, mysterious, delicate, violent

Overflowing with joy, You create myriads
fling galaxies across space, sow them with countless
        kinds of life,

Your love, massive, cosmic, joyful, explodes around us,
as in the beginning, in a burst of light, a rush of waters,
in the cry of birth, in ourselves, even in ourselves.

In the Beginning
Nan Sherman
1985, Los Angeles

Nan Sherman's image of God, the creator, is presented
as a mother.

———————————◆———————————

In the beginning...
a tear
from the Mother's eye,
fell on resistant earth,
splashed to the four winds,
and multiplied. She
heaved a great sigh,
inhaling them skyward. Yet
again She wept
and they fell
as healing rain,
flooding streams into rivers,
rivers into lakes,
inspiring ocean cities,
clean, shimmering,
transparent as crystal,
where the Mother's tears
are golden reflections
seen through watery dreams.

Kiddush Levana
Ruth Finer Mintz
1970, Israel

In this poem of mourning, poet and translator Ruth Finer
Mintz addresses the feminine aspect of God's spirit, the
indwelling presence, *Atikah Kadisha.*

---

blessing the new moon...Haifa, July
for Saul nineteen years, fallen June 1967

A thousand lamps for you in the curve of the shore
shaping below, the blessing,
for the pulse of the sea is the constancy of our longing.
Our masts are for you, torches,
as we stand on the watchtowers of longing.

Come to us out of the shadows, out of the circles of
      mourning.
Lost, lost to parents, to friends. Lost, lost to the
      beloved.

Come to us over water, for the stars are a gust of gulls
      calling.

The sea ablaze is a rim of silver.
The sky ablaze is a rim of crystal.

Return us to yourself and we return
past the cup of salt and sorrow
to You, who are wine and water.

In the open places we set tables.
In flagons of pomegranate we store velvet fire.
For our desire has ripened, apricot and almond.
Our children eat, grow beautiful on the mountain.

Atikah Kadisha, indwelling presence, Mother of Mercies.
Cup of life that is the sea
Arch of life that is the sky
Bow of life that is the shore
Wing of life that is the stars
Blessing of life, the new moon.
Breath of life in our nostrils
Imagination for life, our thoughts
Word of life upon our mouth
                    and acceptable to You

Prayer for Endings
Myra Sklarew
1982, United States

Myra Sklarew incorporates the esoteric Kabalistic concept
of the vessel into this contemporary poem.

———————————•———————————

Let this vessel for water be perfect, without
a broken place. Let its lip be even and unspouted;
we shall pour water from its edge.

And if there is no vessel, let us dip our hands
together into a stream and if the color of the water
has changed, let it be due to natural cause.

If the painter has hands which are covered with dye
or the butcher's with blood or the printer's with ink,
let these not be obstructions; let him wash with us.

And in the morning out of this golden theater
where the shape of wood makes a parabola in the air
mapping out the curve of our life,

let us bury the other in us and all those years
which we opened like a text some faithful teacher
put into our hands for the first time

innocent of its lines and its intersections.
Let us close off in the morning the small valves of the
        heart
and all such doors to those rooms where we once lived.

Prayer
Carol Adler
1981, Cedar Rock

Carol Adler's prayer uses a familiar and frustrating experience
to symbolize her communication with God.

———————————•———————————

I'm writing this
while holding on a long-distance
call to a stranger
and the information I'm asking for
concerns a conversation between two
strangers
that has not yet occurred.

I've waited so long I know I should
hang up but if I do I will lose the
connection and all this time
I've waited will have been in vain

since I will probably have to transmit all of this
once more not to the stranger I'm waiting for
but to someone else
meaning that the whole nature of the
conversation will have to be
altered in order to accommodate not two
but three strangers and not one
but two connections.

I am the stranger holding
and the writer writing
and I am calling you
I am
calling you
calling you
I am

I am

God is portrayed differently in each of these three short poems: the parent, the soul and the unknown.

Everybody's Got Problems
Odeda Rosenthal
1983, New York

God, in heaven, must be lonely—
For we have taken charge at will.
But now and then we pay a visit,
Like to a parent who is ill.

Prayer
Elaine Starkman
1977, Walnut Creek, California

lord, let my soul
soar above my room
let her dance on walls
to songs of violins
leap rooftops
to pages of poetry
praise
       an orange, a horse
       a mountain, a breeze

let her transcend all limits
of my small life

Baruch Hu
Amy K. Blank
1970, Cincinnati

We look into chambers of the Unknown
along a scimitar of light
and say, "Be blessed..."
It is our utmost flight.

Blessing of Tears
Adela Karliner
1982, San Diego

In the traditional liturgy, Jewish men thank God daily for
being born a man. Adela Karliner describes the value of being
a woman.

———————————————

When we gather together to worship as women,
I thank God that I was born a woman.

As we bless each other and the women in our lives,
the tears flow and through them we are connected
by grief, love, joy and insight.

Women connect to each other,
to mothers, grandmothers, foremothers,
to daughters and to granddaughters.
Your grandmother becomes mine
and my daughter becomes yours.

This connection is powerful—
a strong current of feeling
conducted by the medium of our tears.

To some, tears may be a symbol of woman's weakness.
Here they are the symbol of a woman's strength:
her ability to express feeling, empathy, connectedness.

Shechinah, I pray that Your spirit may pervade
those whose tears will not flow; that they may
experience the release of feeling that connects
us to each other, to the tradition of our ancestors,
to our progeny and to all humanity.

For the blessing of tears,
I thank God I was born a woman.

Second Hymn to the Shekhina
Rachel Adler
1980, Minneapolis

Shekhina (Shechinah), the divine presence, is the highest feminine attribute of God's spirit in Kabalistic literature. She has been rediscovered in our search for more universal expression.

———————————•———————————

Daddy says nothing
Comes of nothing. Daddy says
Nothing is a scalding stinking pit
Wet lips like rotten black peonies
Waiting to suck you in.
Pray to Daddygod to save you, Daddy says.

Lady, by all your names,
The lost, the forgotten, the not yet born, I swear
I'll never again
Pray against my own flesh.
Teach me, answer me
Rachel to Rachel
You tell me/I tell you
Nothing is my own mama and
I am nothing myself.

Open my mouth. I'll pray you
A litany of nothing
          hollow in the pot   nothing
          hole in the flute   nothing
          rest in the music   nothing
          shabbat in the week   nothing
          tehom in the universe   nothing
Amen   Imi   Emet

I am your daughter, Lady
And pregnant with you.

Holy wind whistle through me
Been a long time
Since you had a pipe for this music.

Psalm
Lynn Gottlieb
1980, United States

Jewish women, seeking a more personal language for prayer, have explored sources within and outside of Judaism. Rabbi Lynn Gottlieb transforms a psalm of Ishtar to praise God's presence through women's vision.

———————————•■—————————

PRAISE HER
MOST AWESOME OF THE MIGHTY
REVERE HER
SHE IS A WOMAN OF THE PEOPLE
PRAISE HER
SHE IS CLOTHED IN LOVE
SHE IS LADEN WITH VITALITY
HER LIPS ARE SWEET
LIFE IS IN HER MOUTH
WHEN WE SEE HER
OUR REJOICING BECOMES FULL
SHE IS GLORIOUS
SHE IS BEAUTIFUL
HER EYES SHINE LIGHT
SHE IS A WOMAN OF HER PEOPLE
WITH HER IS THEIR COUNSEL
THE FATE OF ALL THINGS SHE HOLDS IN HER HANDS

IN HER PRESENCE COMES ALL CREATION
THE CREATION OF JOY—STRENGTH—WISDOM—CARING
WORLDS AND WORLDS SPUN OUT OF HER VISION
SHE PROTECTS THE DAY AND GUARDS THE NIGHT
SHE KEEPS THE CYCLES FLOWING
SHE IS A SLAVE—A VIRGIN—A MOTHER—A CRONE
SHE IS ALL WOMEN—SHE IS FREEDOM
SHE IS THE PARTING SEAS
THE GIFT OF LIGHT
THE ORACLE—THE WOMB OF COMPASSION
POWER IS IN HER HAND

LOVE IS IN HER HEART
CREATION IS IN HER BEING
SHECHINAH—MALCHUT SHAMAYIM

TEHOMOT—ELAT
ACHOTI CALAH
YAH TZVOAT—EL SHADDAI
EMHAMRACHAMIM
SHABBAT CHAI OLAMIN
PRAISE HER WHEN YOU COME UPON HER NAME
SINGING INSIDE YOU
SHE IS THE BREATH OF ALL LIVING
PRAISE HER
REVERE HER
THERE IS POWER IN HER HAND
THERE IS LOVE IN HER HEART
PRAISE HER

A Kiddush for New Holidays
Marcia Falk
1984, Los Angeles

In her new blessing Marcia Falk has incorporated traditional Jewish symbols and imagery which broaden and enrich our vision of God and prayer and, prophetically, transcend sexuality.

N'varekh et ein ha-ḥayyim
matzmiḥat p'ri ha-gafen
v'nishzor et s'rigei ḥayyeinu
b'masoret ha-am.

Let us bless the source of life
that ripens fruit on the vines
as we weave the branches of our lives
into the tradition.

N'varekh et ma'yan ḥayyeinu
sheheḥeyanu v'kiyy'manu v'higgianu
la-z'man ha-zeh.

Let us bless the flow of life
that revives us, sustains us,
and brings us to this time.

This book is not complete until the reader adds here her own voice and prayers.

Sources

The following collections are good sources for the reader who is interested in reading more poetry by Jewish women.

Ausubel, Nathan and Maryann. *A Treasury of Jewish Poetry*. New York: Crown Publishers, 1957.

Bankier, Joanne, Carol Cosman, *et al. The Other Voice*. New York: W. W. Norton and Co., 1976.

Betsky, Sarah Zweig. *Onions and Cucumbers and Plums*. Detroit: Wayne State University Press, 1958.

Dworkin, Marc. *Shirim: A Jewish Poetry Journal,* published semi-annually. Los Angeles: Hillel Extension, 900 Hilgard Ave.

Glazer, Myra. *Burning Air and a Clear Mind: Contemporary Israeli Women Poets*. Athens, Ohio: Ohio University Press, 1981.

Howe, Florence and Ellen Bass. *No More Masks*. Garden City, N.Y.: Anchor Press, 1973.

Howe, Irving and Eliezer Greenberg. *A Treasury of Yiddish Poetry*. New York: Holt, Rinehart, and Winston, 1969.

Leftwich, Joseph. *The Golden Peacock*. New York: Thomas Yoseloff, 1961.

Lifshin, Lynn. *Tangled Vines: A Collection of Mother and Daughter Poems*. Boston: Beacon Press, 1978.

Schwartz, Howard and Anthony Rudolph, editors. *Voices within the Ark: The Modern Jewish Poets*. New York: Avon Books, 1980.

Spiegel, Marcia Cohn. *The Jewish Woman: A Portrait in Her Own Words*. (A dramatic reading.) New York: National Federation of Temple Sisterhoods, 1979.

Permissions

The dates attributed to each poem reflect the year of publication.

"Monologues with God" by Miriam Kubovy is published with permission of the *Jewish Spectator,* March 1964.

"The Song of Deborah and Barak" and "Hannah's Prayer" are from *The Holy Scriptures: According to the Masoretic Text.* Jewish Publication Society, Philadelphia, 1917.

"Judith's Song of Thanksgiving" is from *Apocrypha and Pseudigrapha,* Clarendon Press, Oxford, England, 1913.

"There is a City" by Sambetha, "Prayer Before Sleep" by Alice Lucas, "My Inmost Hope" by Sarah Copia Sullam, and "Passionate Sword" by Jean Starr Untermeyer are from *A Treasury of Jewish Poetry,* edited by Nathan and Maryann Ausubel, Crown Publishers, New York, 1957.

"With the Help of God" by Roselle Fishels, "Prayer" by Galah, and "Prayer for Sabbath" by Chana Katz appeared in Yiddish in *Anthology of Yiddish Women's Poetry,* edited by E. Corman, Chicago, 1928, and were translated by Mahlia Lynn Schubert.

"Prayer" by Deborah Ascarelli was translated from Hebrew by Avshalom Cohen.

"Then We'll Be Privileged" by Rachel Morpurgo is from *Written out of History*, by Sondra Henry and Emily Taitz, Biblio Press, New York, 1983.

"I Never Loved a Flower" by Grace Aguilar is from *The Spirit of Judaism*, Sherman and Co., Philadelphia, 1873.

"Prayer on the Approach of Accouchement" by Fanny Neuda is from *Hours of Devotion*, translated from German by M. Mayer, L. H. Frank, New York, 1878.

"All Right in the End" by Abbie Hatch and "Psalms" by Minnie Louis are from *The American Jewess*.

"To God" by Else Lasker-Schüler is from *Hebrew Ballads and Other Poems*, Jewish Publication Society, Philadelphia, 1980.

"The Maabaroth" by Rikudah Potash is from *The Golden Peacock*, edited by Joseph Leftwich, Thomas Yoseloff, New York, 1961.

"I Know Not Your Way" by Malka Heifetz Tussman is from *Am I also You*, Tree Books, Berkeley, 1977, and is translated from Yiddish by Marcia Falk.

"In Your Image" by Shulamis Yelin is from *Seeded in Sinai*, Reconstruction Press, New York, 1975, and is also available in French translation as *Au Soleil de ma Nuit*, Les Editions Fides, Montreal, 1975.

"How Long Have We Forgotten How to Listen" by Nelly Sachs is from *The Seekers*, 1970, Farrar, Straus and Giroux, New York.

"Daughters of Israel" by Peninah Moise is from *Secular and Religious Work,* Nicholas Duffy, Charleston, South Carolina, 1911.

"Sabbath Eve" by Jessie Sampter is from *Brand Plucked from the Fire,* Jewish Publication Society, Philadelphia, 1937.

"Friday Night" by Karen Gershon is from *Selected Poems,* Harcourt Brace and World, New York, 1966.

"The Sabbath" by Charlotte Anker is from *Reconstructionist,* October, 1966.

"Suburban Shabbes" by Brenda Gevertz is from *Jewish Spectator,* Fall 1974.

"Friday Night Cantata" by Florence Victor is from *Commentary,* Vol. 26, 1958.

"Friday Night" by Diane Levenberg is from *Out of the Desert,* Doubleday, New York, 1980.

"Kabbalat Shabbat" by Sandy Eisenberg Sasso is from *Reconstructionist,* June 1974.

"If God Had Known" by Hortense Flexner is from the *Menorah Journal,* 1919.

"Disquisition" by Chana Bloch is from *Midstream,* Vol. 13, 1967.

"Questions" by Bea Stadtler is from *The Jewish Spectator,* 1964.

"God of Mercy" by Kadia Molodowsky, translated by Irving Howe, and "If" by Rosa Gutman Jasny, translated by Etta Blum are from *A Treasury of Yiddish Poetry.*

"Sinai" by Joanne Seltzer is from *Waterways,* 1985.

"Kol Nidre" by Rosa Felsenburg Kaplan is published in full in *Shirim,* Fall 1982.

"Faith and Reason" by Lillian Ott is from *The Jewish Spectator,* Vol. 26, December 1961.

"Genesis" by Ruth Brin is from *The Jewish Spectator,* Vol. 29, January 1964.

"Kiddush Levana" by Ruth Finer Mintz is from *Jerusalem Poems, Love Songs,* Massada Press, Jerusalem, 1976.

"Prayer for Endings" by Myra Sklarew is from *The Science of Goodbyes,* University of Georgia Press, 1982.

"Everybody's Got Problems" by Odeda Rosenthal is from *I Never Said I was a Lady,* 1982.

"Blessing of Tears" by Adela Karliner is from *On Our Spiritual Journey,* Woman's Institute for Continuing Jewish Education, San Diego, 1984.

"Psalm" by Lynn Gottlieb is from *Response,* 1980.

"A Kiddush for New Holidays" by Marcia Falk is from *Moment,* March, 1985.

About the Editors

Marcia Cohn Spiegel, M.A., Hebrew Union College—Jewish Institute of Religion, teaches women's studies in the Department of Continuing Education at the University of Judaism, where she explores the development of contemporary issues through Jewish historical, sociological, and literary sources.

Deborah Lipton Kremsdorf, M.A., teaches secondary school math and science in San Diego, California. She is active in the Reconstructionist movement. She is married to a physician and has an eight-year-old daughter.